D0119671

CHILDREN'S ATLAS OF IRELAND

Theodore Rowland-Entwistle
and
Clare Oliver

First published in 2000 by
Miles Kelly Publishing Ltd
Bardfield Centre, Great Bardfield, Essex, CM7 4SL

2 4 6 8 10 9 7 5 3 1

Editor: Clare Oliver
Designer: Sally Boothroyd
Project Manager: Kate Miles
Art Director: Clare Sleven
Editorial Director: Paula Borton
Production: Rachel Jones
Artwork Commissioning: Susanne Grant, Lynne French, Natasha Smith
Picture Research: Janice Bracken, Lesley Cartlidge, Liberty Newton
Cartography: Digital Wisdom
Index: Lynn Bresler
Repro House: DPI
Additonal help from Ian Paulyn & Jane Walker

British Library Cataloguing-in-Publication Data
A catalogue record for this book is available from the British Library

ISBN 1-902947-52-5

Printed in Hong Kong

CAN YOU FIND?

Look out for these boxes as you read this book. They suggest places to look for on the regional maps. Why not see if you can use the lettered and numbered borders on the map pages to work out map co-ordinates for each place? You can find out how to use map co-ordinates on page 30. And on page 32 you will find answers for all the 'Can You Find?' locations, written as co-ordinates.

MAP ICONS

Look out for the icons on the maps. They show where there are special features. They represent:

Airports

Castles

Cathedrals and Abbeys

Forestry

Leisure and Pleasure

Ports

Stately homes

Contents

About map icons & Can You Find? 4

Contents 5

IRELAND: INTRODUCTION 6

Ireland: Physical features 8

Belfast 10

Northern Ireland 12

Dublin 16

Connacht 18

Leinster 20

Munster 24

Ulster 28

Index 31

Acknowledgements 32

Can You Find? answers 32

Ireland

◀ Shamrock
The shamrock, or wood sorrel, is Ireland's national flower.

◀ Irish harp
The Irish harp, around since medieval times, is often used as a symbol of the country itself.

IRELAND IS THE SECOND-LARGEST ISLAND of the British Isles. Its southern part forms the Republic of Ireland. The northeast corner is the province of Northern Ireland, which is part of the United Kingdom. Historically, Ireland was divided into the four provinces of Connacht, Leinster, Munster and Ulster. Six of the nine counties of Ulster form Northern Ireland, and the other three are in the Republic.

▲ Patron saint of Ireland
The feast day of Ireland's patron saint, St Patrick, falls on March 17th. On that day, Irish people wear green, their national colour.

In its early days Ireland was torn by wars between rival kings, whom Viking settlers were unable to control. In 1166 the king of Leinster, Dermot MacMurrough, travelled to Wales and appealed to a Norman baron, nicknamed Strongbow, for help against his enemies. Strongbow married Dermot's daughter, and in 1171 succeeded him as king of Leinster. Strongbow in turn appealed for help to the English king, Henry II. Henry tried to conquer the country. Seven centuries of struggle followed, culminating in the 1801 Act of Union which made Ireland part of the United Kingdom.

Struggle for freedom

The 19th century was a time of great poverty and hardship in Ireland. Increasingly the Irish demanded Home Rule. Although this was promised, it was postponed because of World War I. Beginning in 1916, the Irish people took power by force, and won some independence in 1922. Nearly all the Irish were Roman Catholics. The Protestant majority in the northeast chose to remain part of the United Kingdom. Southern Ireland was at first a Free State, with the British monarch as its nominal head of state. In 1949 it declared itself an independent republic, with the name of Eire, the Gaelic for Ireland.

▼ British soldiers
From 1972, British soldiers were posted in Northern Ireland to help the police to control terrorism.

The Republic of Ireland

The Republic of Ireland's government consists of a president, a parliament with two houses, a prime minister and a cabinet. The president is head of state, with mainly ceremonial duties. The parliament consists of an upper house and a lower house, called Dáil Éireann. The Dáil, the main law-making body, has 166 elected members. Parliament meets in Leinster House. Local government is in the hands of 27 county councils.

◀ Roman Catholicism
The Republic of Ireland's official religion is Roman Catholicism. Believers buy candles and light them in church as an offering to God.

Northern Ireland

Northern Ireland is a province of the United Kingdom. It had its own parliament and administration, founded in 1921, but sections of the population did not want to remain part of the United Kingdom. In 1969 the Provisional IRA (Irish Republican Army) began a terrorist campaign with the aim of Northern Ireland joining the Republic.

To maintain control, the British government suspended the Northern Ireland Parliament, and began to rule the province directly from Westminster. Much of the life of the province divided along religious lines, with the Roman Catholic minority in opposition to the Protestant majority. Although most ordinary people wished to live in peace, some sections of both communities formed paramilitary organizations in violent opposition to the British government and its policies.

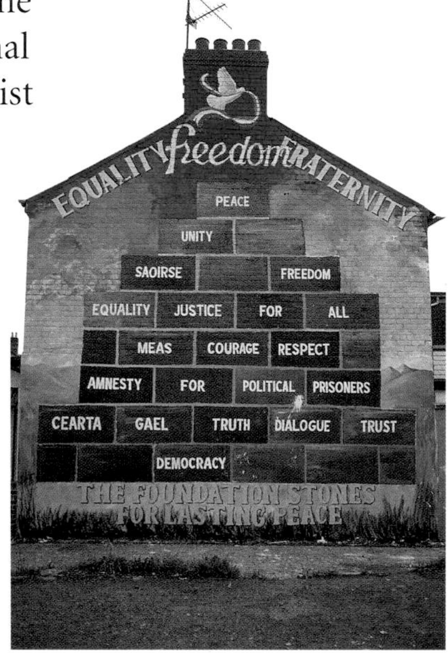

▲ Political slogans
The buildings of Belfast bear the mark of decades of political unrest, with many slogans and murals.

COUNTRY FACTS

NORTHERN IRELAND
Area: 14,121 sq km
Population: 1,595,000
Capital: Belfast
Other cities: Bangor, Londonderry (Derry), Newtownabbey
Official language: English
Main religions: Protestantism, Roman Catholicism
Currency: Pound sterling (£)
Highest point: Slieve Donard (852 m)
Longest river: Upper and Lower Bann (137 km)
Largest lake: Lough Neagh (396 sq km)

REPUBLIC OF IRELAND
Area: 70,284 sq km
Population: 3,590,000
Capital: Dublin
Major cities: Cork, Dún Laoghaire, Limerick, Waterford
Official languages: English, Irish Gaelic
Main religions: Roman Catholicism, Protestantism
Currency: Punt (Euro from year 2002)
Highest point: Carrauntoohill (1,041 m)
Longest river: Shannon (370 km)
Largest lake: Lough Corrib (176 sq km)

CUCHULAIN

To this day, poets are inspired by the myths of Ireland, which include tales of many great heroes. Cuchulain was one, said to have lived during the 1st century BC. He was the son of the god Lug, and a fierce warrior. His strength was superhuman and even the most vile monsters ran away from him! According to legend, he defeated whole armies single-handed – including that of Queen Maeve of Connacht when he was just 17 years old. Cuchulain was as handsome as he was brave, but he easily flew into a rage. He is said to have died, aged 27, after being tricked by his enemies.

The road to peace

In 1985 the Dublin and Westminster governments signed an Anglo-Irish agreement, giving the Irish government an advisory role in Northern Ireland's affairs. Fresh efforts to reach a settlement began in 1997, and in 1998 the Republican and Loyalist organizations agreed to stop violence. In 1998 Roman Catholic and Protestant members were elected to a new assembly, with a view to forming a new government for the province.

Ireland
Physical features

IRELAND IS SEPARATED FROM GREAT BRITAIN by the Irish Sea. At Torr Head, County Antrim, Ireland is only 22 kilometres away from the Mull of Kintyre in Scotland. The main features of Ireland's landscape are its rolling plains, its mountains and its coastline. Ireland is often called the 'Emerald Isle' because of its wide expanses of picturesque green lowland.

▲ **Northern pike**
Ireland's rivers and lakes are home to salmon, trout, pike, bream, perch and roach.

The centre of the island is a broad, low plain, which consists mostly of farmland with some woodlands and peat bogs. Scattered mountains and highland regions lie near the coasts, notably the Plateau of Antrim and the Mourne Mountains in the northeast, the Donegal Mountains in the northwest, the Wicklow Mountains in the southeast, and the Mountains of Mayo, Connemara and Kerry in the west.

▲ **Boggy harvest**
Over many thousands of years, large areas of peat bogs have formed in Ireland. Peat is the rotted remains of ancient vegetation. It is cut and dried to make fuel.

The coastline along the Irish Sea is smooth compared to Ireland's west coast. Pounded by Atlantic waves and storms, the west coast is a mass of deep bays and inlets, with high, rocky cliffs. The river Shannon, the longest in the British Isles, empties into the Atlantic Ocean. The largest of Ireland's many lakes, which are mostly in the west of the island, is Lough Neagh, in Northern Ireland.

▼ **River Shannon**
The Shannon is edged by marshland for much of its 370-km course. It drains an area of over 15,500 sq km.

▼ **Rocky cliffs**
Donegal, in the northwest of Ireland, faces the powerful Atlantic Ocean. Its dramatic, jagged cliffs have been weathered over millions of years.

Rocks of Ireland

Like Great Britain, Ireland was once part of two separate, ancient continents. If you imagine a diagonal line from Berwick-upon-Tweed, England, to the mouth of the river Shannon, that is where the two continents came together (see pages 68–69). Everything north of the line on both islands was originally part of a continent which continued into North America. A long-vanished ocean separated it from the land that is now England and the southern part of Ireland. As a result, the rocks of Northern Ireland are a continuation of those found in Scotland. The hills of western Galway and Counties Mayo and Londonderry were originally a continuation of the Scottish Highlands.

▲ **Wicklow mountains**
Shrouded in mist, this chain rises in County Wicklow, Leinster. Long ago, glaciers scraped and smoothed the hills, exposing the underlying granite.

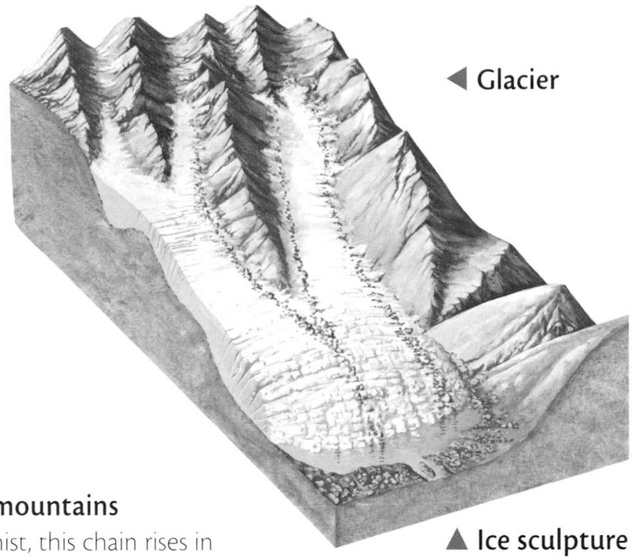

▲ **Ice sculpture**
Glaciers shaped the Irish landscape during the last Ice Age, 10,000 years ago.

A lot of these hills have a foundation of granite, an igneous (volcanic) rock. The extraordinary rock formation of the Giant's Causeway, County Antrim, is similar to the rock columns at Fingal's Cave, on the island of Staffa in the Inner Hebrides. Both formations were part of the same volcanic eruption. When the hot, liquid rock flooded out of the Earth's interior, it cooled to form amazing six-sided columns, or pillars, of a black rock called basalt.

Cut off by the sea

The Irish Sea formed thousands of years before Great Britain was separated from continental Europe. When animals and plants reached the British Isles from continental Europe, some species did not reach the island of Ireland before it was cut off from Great Britain. Examples include snakes, moles, voles and common shrews.

▲ **Emerald Isle**
Green is Ireland's national colour. The fields glow green, thanks to plentiful rains brought by the prevailing winds across the Atlantic.

CLIMATE

Ireland's climate is mild and damp and there are few sharp frosts or heavy snowfalls. Its mildness is due to the North Atlantic Drift, a current that brings the warm waters of the Gulf Stream to northwestern Europe. The rains are brought to Ireland by a series of depressions (low-pressure systems) which are carried across the Atlantic by the prevailing winds. Most of the island has 762–1,270 mm of rain a year. The highest rainfall occurs in western Connacht and County Kerry, where it can reach 2,286–2,540 mm. As in England, the sunniest part of the island is the southeastern corner.

▼ **Giant's Causeway**
Some of these rocky, hexagonal pillars of basalt in County Antrim are up to six metres high and half a metre across.

▲ **The Burren**
Rocky outcrops of limestone dot the landscape of the Burren in County Clare. It is home to some unique alpine plants.

Belfast

▶ **Custom House**
An essential building in any busy port, Belfast's Custom House is on the waterfront.

BELFAST HAS BEEN THE CAPITAL of Northern Ireland since 1920, when the province first became separated from the southern part of the island. It is the largest city in the province, with a population of 296,300. Belfast stands on the river Lagan, at the head of Belfast Lough, a large bay facing towards Scotland. It is a seaport and Northern Ireland's leading industrial centre.

Belfast's linen-weaving is a historic industry. Shipbuilding began in the late 18th century, and is still one of Belfast's main industries. A huge aircraft factory was established in 1937.

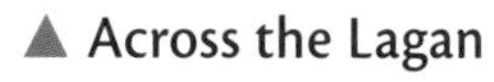

▲ **Across the Lagan**
Queen's Bridge was built by Sir Charles Lanyon. Completed in 1843, it is named after Queen Victoria.

▼ **Shipbuilding**
The ill-fated *Titanic* was made by Belfast shipbuilders. The city's shipyards line the eastern shores of Belfast Lough.

Important buildings

Belfast has some fine buildings, many dating from the late 1800s and early 1900s. Others have been built since World War II. (Enemy bombing destroyed much of the city in 1941, with the loss of 1,000 lives.) The heart of the city is Donegall Square, where City Hall stands.

▲ **Belfast Castle**
The castle grounds feature mosaic cats, sculpture and garden furniture. There's a legend that the castle residents will have good luck if a white cat lives there.

Other notable landmarks in the city centre are the Royal Courts of Justice and St Anne's Cathedral. The Ulster Museum is set in the picturesque surroundings of the city's Botanic Gardens. In the eastern suburb of Stormont is Parliament House. The governmental Northern Ireland Office is based in nearby Stormont Castle. Northern Ireland has two universities: Queen's University, which dates from 1908 and is the province's largest; and the University of Ulster, which was formed in 1984 and has campuses in Belfast, Coleraine and Londonderry.

PLACES OF INTEREST

ART GALLERIES
Malone House, Old Museum Arts Centre, Ormeau Baths Gallery

PARKS
Cavehill Country Park, Lady Dixon Park, Ormeau Park

PLACES OF WORSHIP
Crescent Church, First Presbyterian Church, Moravian Church, St Anne's Cathedral, St Malachy's. St Mary's, St Matthew's

MUSEUMS
Ulster Museum

OTHER ATTRACTIONS
Albert Memorial Clocktower, Belfast Zoo, Botanic Gardens, Lagan Lookout Visitor Centre

▲ **City Hall**
A central landmark is City Hall, Donegall Square. The Renaissance-style building was completed in 1906.

Moments in history

The earliest fact we know about Belfast is that in the 1170s a Norman baron, John de Courci, built a castle by a ford across the river. It became known as Beal Feirste, meaning 'the approach to the crossing.' De Courci conquered Ulster, but his castle did not survive. In 1611 Sir Arthur Chichester, Lord Deputy of Ireland, built a new 'stately palace.' Fire destroyed Chichester's castle in 1708, but the town surrounding it grew and thrived. Belfast's main industry was the spinning and weaving of linen from local-grown flax, and this had expanded in the 1600s following the arrival of French Huguenot (Protestant) refugees, who were expert weavers. By 1800 the city was home to 20,000 people; today, it has a population of over 362,000. Belfast's recent history has been dominated by political conflict. Street riots during 1969 led to the introduction of British troops in 1972. The rest of the 20th century saw terrorism on both sides, but a Peace Agreement in 1999 provided new hope for the city's future.

◀ **Glasshouse**
The impressive, iron-framed Palm House, built between 1839 and 1852, is the centrepiece of Belfast's Botanic Gardens.

◀ **Belfast streets**
The cityscape is dominated by rows and rows of terraced houses, and by the river Lagan.

▲ **Stormont Castle**
The Northern Ireland Parliament met at Stormont from 1932 until 1972. There are hopes that the new Northern Ireland Assembly will meet here.

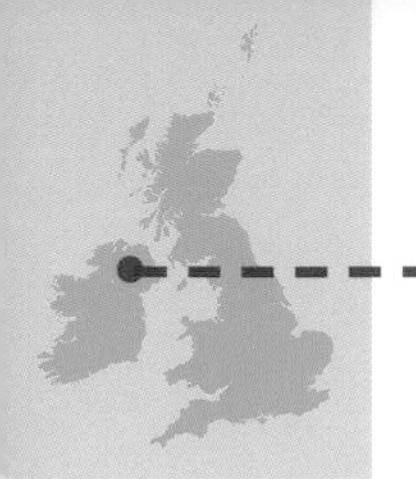

Northern Ireland

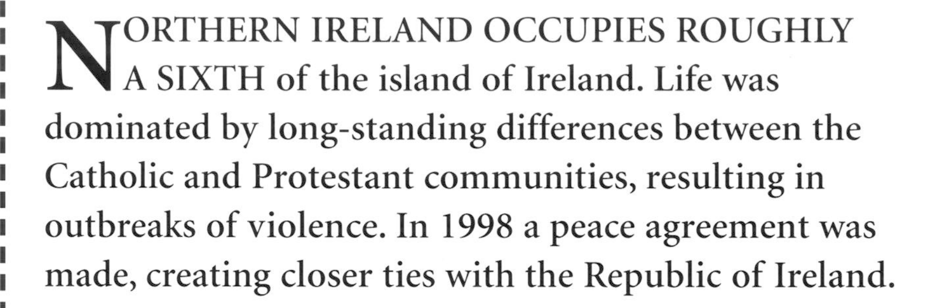

NORTHERN IRELAND OCCUPIES ROUGHLY A SIXTH of the island of Ireland. Life was dominated by long-standing differences between the Catholic and Protestant communities, resulting in outbreaks of violence. In 1998 a peace agreement was made, creating closer ties with the Republic of Ireland.

The landscape is characterized by fertile, rolling plains and low mountain ranges, which are often close to the coastline. In the west, the thinly-populated Sperrin Mountains form a crescent running almost to the sea at Coleraine in the north. In the northeast, the high plateau of the Mountains of Antrim is cut by deep glens. In the southeast, the Mourne Mountains contain the region's highest peak, Slieve Donard (852 metres). Flanking the river Mourne in Tyrone are two hills, Bessy Bell and Mary Gray. They are named after two Scotswomen who died of plague in Perth in 1666.

Lakes and rivers

The region has several freshwater lakes, of which Lough Neagh is the most important. It covers 396 square kilometres and is the largest lake in the British Isles. The longest river is the river Bann, which is really two rivers – the Upper Bann and the Lower Bann. The river Foyle forms part of the western border with the Irish Republic.

Important towns

Two-thirds of the population live in cities and towns. The largest cities are Belfast and Londonderry. Belfast is a university town and Northern Ireland's main seaport, operating ferry services to other ports in Northern Ireland and to the west coasts of England and Scotland. The city also has an international airport.

▼ Stepping stones
According to legend, a giant called Finn MacCool built the Giant's Causeway so that he could walk to Scotland without getting his feet wet! It consists of over 40,000 hexagonal columns of volcanic rock, called basalt.

▼ County Down
The Mourne Mountains are topped with dark, craggy peaks of granite. The beautiful Silent Valley cuts through the mountains.

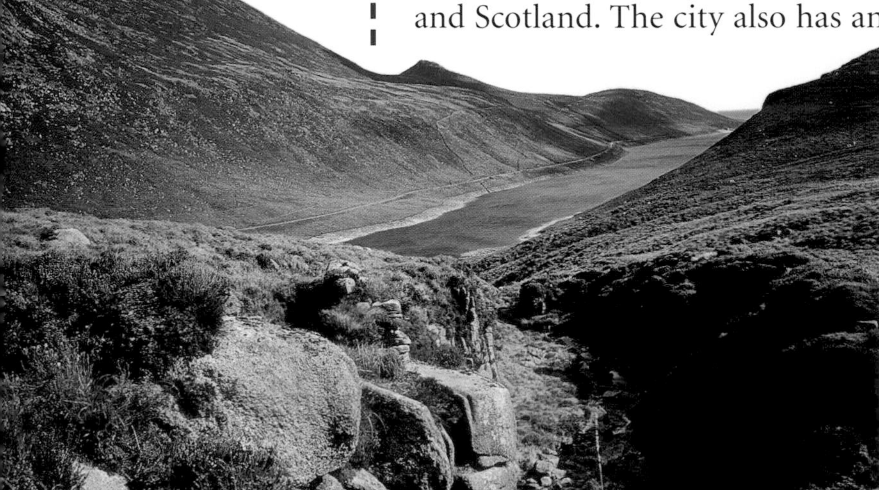

▲ Sticky trick
This carnivorous plant is native to Ireland's bogs, as found in County Tyrone. It sets a gummy trap for passing insects.

▲ Statue of hope
This monument in Londonderry is called 'Hands across the Divide.' The 1998 peace agreement led to hopes for greater tolerance between Protestants and Catholics.

DODOS & DINOS
The gardens at Mount Stewart House, County Down, are populated by strange statues. They include mermaids, platypuses, dinosaurs and dodos.

COUNTY FACTS

COUNTY ANTRIM
Area: 2,832 sq km
Key places: Antrim, Ballycastle, Ballymena, Bushmills, Carrickfergus

COUNTY ARMAGH
Area: 1,254 sq km
Key places: Armagh, Portadown

BELFAST DISTRICT
Area: 65 sq km
Key place: Belfast

COUNTY DOWN
Area: 2,448 sq km
Adminstrative centre: Downpatrick
Other key places: Banbridge, Bangor, Newry, Newtownards

COUNTY FERMANAGH
Area: 1,676 sq km
Key place: Enniskillen

COUNTY LONDONDERRY
Area: 2,077 sq km
Key places: Coleraine, Limavady, Portstewart

LONDONDERRY CITY DISTRICT
Area: 8.8 sq km
Key place: Londonderry

COUNTY TYRONE
Area: 3,137 sq km
Key places: Cookstown, Dungannon, Omagh

Wildlife havens

Strangford Lough is a naturalists' paradise, with flocks of ducks, geese and wading birds, as well as large numbers of basking seals. Birds of prey, such as buzzards and peregrines, are a regular sight along the northern stretch of coastline known as White Park Bay. Further south, in the Sperrin Mountains, sika deer can be spotted in the Gortin Glen Forest Park. Huge numbers of wildfowl, including great crested grebes, spend their winter in the reedbeds of Lough Neagh.

▲ Reedbed

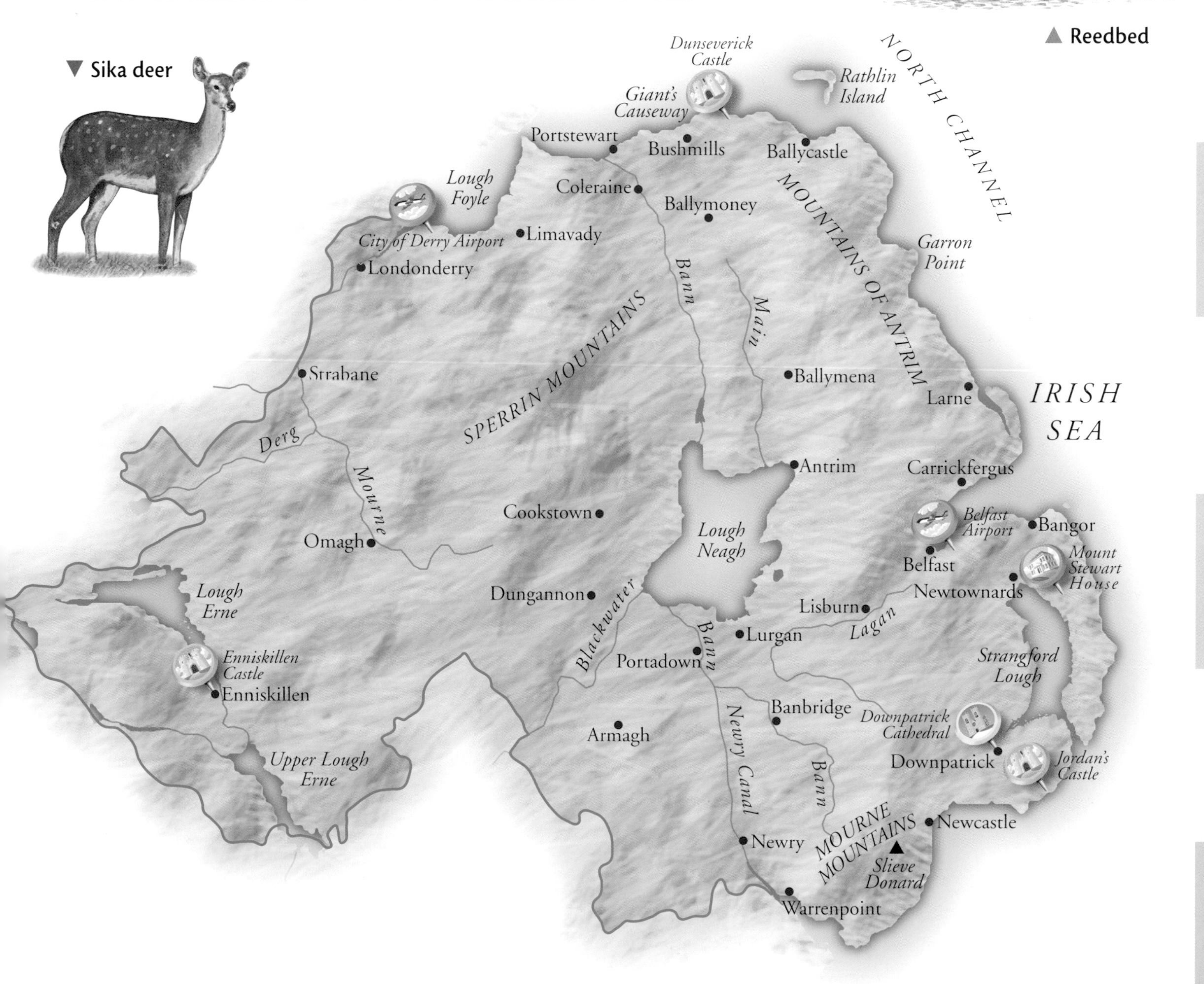

▲ **Legananny Dolmen**
This monument in County Down dates back to Stone Age times.

THE EARLIEST INHABITANTS of Northern Ireland were Stone Age people, who left huge burial chambers and large standing stones. For a long time, their burial chambers were believed to be the graves of giants.

The earliest rulers are mostly legendary ones, but they were probably based on real people. Two thousand years ago there was a Kingdom of Ulster. The ruins of its capital, Emain Macha, lie near present-day Armagh Town. According to legend, the ruler of Ulster was Conor MacNessa, who had an army known as the Knights of the Red Branch. Its greatest warrior was Cuchulain, said to be the son of the sun god Lug. In the AD300s a king named Niall of the Nine Hostages formed a kingdom in the west of Northern Ireland. At about that time many of the region's people were Scots, who later invaded Scotland and settled there.

PATRON SAINT

St Patrick brought Christianity to Ireland in the 5th century. According to legend, he drove all the snakes from Ireland into the sea. Patrick's grave is said to be in the grounds of Down Cathedral in Downpatrick. Two cathedrals in Armagh City honour the saint: St Patrick's Church of Ireland Cathedral and St Patrick's Roman Catholic Cathedral.

Protestants in Northern Ireland

The English made several attempts to conquer Northern Ireland, but were fiercely resisted. From 1610 onwards the British rulers began what is called the plantation of Ireland, encouraging English and Scottish people to move there. This introduced a number of Protestants into an island which, until then, had been completely Roman Catholic.

▲ **March of the Orangemen**
In the late 17th century there was a war between the ousted Roman Catholic king, James II of England, and his Protestant successor, William III of Orange. In support of William, the apprentice boys of Londonderry shut the city gates to keep out James's armies. To this day, Protestant political groups, known as Orange Lodges, have celebrated with a marching season that lasts from Easter until July 12th.

▼ **Ancient prayer book**
The *Antiphonary of Bangor* is a prayer book that dates back to the AD600s. It is all that remains of the monastery at Bangor, County Down, which was sacked by the Vikings and abandoned in the 11th century.

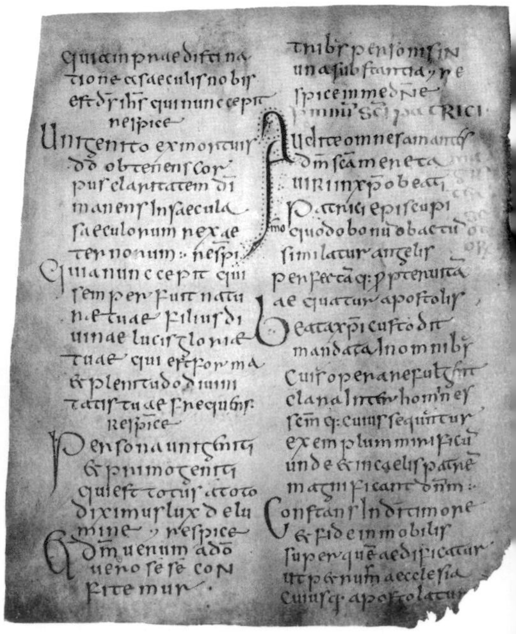

▲ **Making linen**
Huguenot weavers arrived in Northern Ireland in the 1600s and by the 1800s, Belfast was nicknamed Linenopolis. To break down the harvested flax, it was beaten, and then 'scutched' (*left*) with a large knife. Then it was ready to be woven on the loom (*right*).

Castles

Jordan's Castle in County Down was built in the late 1300s and is virtually undamaged. The cliff-top ruins of Dunseverick Castle stand on the north coast of County Antrim. It was once the most fortified castle in the whole of Ireland. The castle was razed by Oliver Cromwell's English soldiers in the 1600s. Nearby is the famous Carrick-a-Rede rope bridge, which links the mainland to a rocky island where there are salmon fisheries. Both Dromore and Clough are motte-and-bailey castles dating from Norman times.

Industry

Light industry, including rayon production, linen weaving and computer manufacture, are among the chief activities in Northern Ireland. There is heavy industry, such as shipbuilding and aircraft manufacture, in and around Belfast. Near Lower Lough Erne is the village of Belleek, famous for its delicate, shiny pottery. A dam near the village provides hydroelectric power. The tiny town of Bushmills in County Antrim is home to the world's oldest distillery.

Farming

Farmers in Northern Ireland export food to the rest of the British Isles. Sheep farming is the main activity in the northeast. In the valley of the river Laggan, between counties Antrim and Down, farmers rear pigs and dairy herds, and grow oats and potatoes.

▲ **Potato plant**

WHAT'S IN A NAME?

ANTRIM
The Gaelic *Aontroim* means 'one house.'

ARMAGH
This county is named after an Irish warrior goddess, Macha.

COUNTY DOWN
Down is named after the town of Downpatrick, which means 'St Patrick's dún,' or fort.

FERMANAGH
The Gaelic *Fear Manach* means 'district of the monks.'

LONDONDERRY
The original name, Derry, means 'oak wood.' St Columba founded a monastery in a nearby oak grove in AD546. In 1613 Londoners settled there so the name changed to Londonderry.

TYRONE
Tír Eoghain means 'land belonging to Eoghain.' Eoghain was the son of a 5th-century High King of Ireland.

▲ **Whiskey vats**
The Bushmills distillery in County Antrim has been making whiskey since 1608.

CAN YOU FIND?

1 Armagh
2 Belfast
3 Bushmills
4 Downpatrick Cathedral
5 Slieve Donard

see page 13

Dublin

DUBLIN IS THE CAPITAL of the Republic of Ireland. It was founded by the Vikings in the 9th century on a hill overlooking the river Liffey. They called its harbour the Black Pool – in Irish Gaelic, 'dubh linn.' The city's official name now is Baile Atha Cliath – 'Ford of the Hurdles.' Dublin is Ireland's largest city and its leading port. It is famed for its handsome architecture, wide streets and large squares.

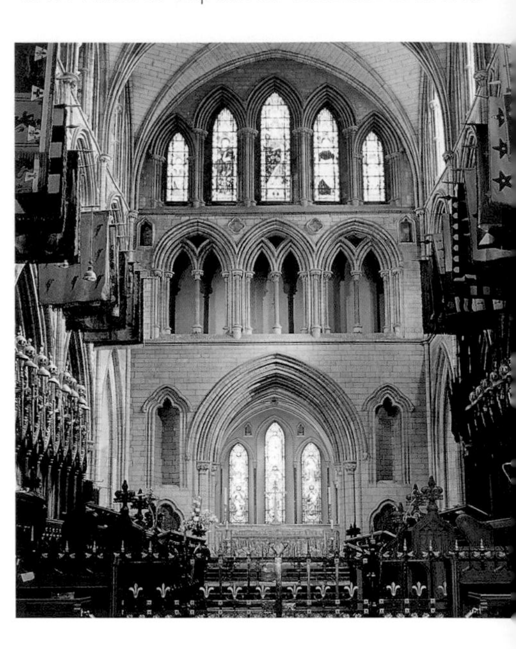

▼ St Patrick's Cathedral
St Patrick's is said to stand on the site of an ancient well. Here, Ireland's patron saint drew water to baptize his Christian converts.

▲ Dublin's bridges
Fourteen bridges span the Liffey in the city, joining the north and south. The river flows through scenic Phoenix Park.

Dublin is the centre of Ireland's road and rail networks. Dublin Airport is at Collinstown, to the north of the city. The city's manufacturing industries include chemicals, clothing, electronics, tobacco and brewing. The service sector plays an important part in the city's economy, and Dublin is a major banking and financial centre.

Important buildings

Dublin has many fine buildings. They include Dublin Castle, the nextdoor City Hall, the Four Courts (law courts), the Custom House, the General Post Office and the Abbey Theatre. Some buildings were damaged in the Easter Rising of 1916, and in the Civil War of 1922–3, but they have all been restored. The city's main shopping area lies along and around Grafton Street and O'Connell Street. At 46 metres wide, O'Connell Street is one of the widest in Europe. Christ Church Cathedral was founded in 1038 within the old walls of the city. St Patrick's Cathedral, which is outside the the old city walls, was begun in 1190. Both of these cathedrals are Anglican (Protestant). The Roman Catholic Metropolitan Pro-Cathedral was built in 1816. There are three universities. The University of Dublin, for which only one college was ever completed, is known as Trinity College, Dublin.

▼ Custom House
Flames claimed Dublin's Custom House in 1921, but it has been restored following James Gandon's original design of the 1780s. The copper dome features four clocks and is topped by a statue of Hope.

▲ Government Buildings
Opened in 1911, these buildings contain the Taoiseach's (Prime Minister's) office and the cabinet rooms.

Moments in history

Although the Irish occupied the city several times, it remained principally in Viking hands until 1170, when it was finally captured by Normans from England. Two years later King Henry II made Dublin the centre of his attempted conquest of Ireland. But the conquest was limited, and for centuries the English territory was confined to an area around Dublin, which became known as the English Pale (boundary). Its people were mostly Protestants. In 1649, during the English Civil War, Dublin was captured by the Parliamentary army of Oliver Cromwell. At that time it had a population of 9,000.

▲ Dublin streets
The Liffey cuts across the city streets down to Portobello Harbour.

During the 1700s Dublin grew and prospered, and by 1800 it was second only to London among the cities of the British Empire. Ireland had its own parliament, based in Dublin in a building that is now the Bank of Ireland. A viceroy represented the British monarch. The Act of Union in 1801 abolished the parliament.

◀ Parnell Square
The square's central statue by Oisin Kelly shows the Children of Lir, the Celtic sea god. They represented the powers of evil.

After the establishment of the Republic of Ireland in 1922, Dublin was racked by the Civil War. Regeneration of the city did not come about until the Republic of Ireland joined the European Union in 1973. Since then, many new buildings and businesses have sprung up.

▲ Trinity College
Elizabeth I founded Dublin's university in 1592. Its Old Library houses the *Book of Kells*.

▼ The DART
The Dublin Area Rapid Transport is an overground rail service that links different parts of the city.

PLACES OF INTEREST

ART GALLERIES
City Arts Centre, Irish Museum of Modern Art, Municipal Gallery of Modern Art, National Gallery

PARKS
Phoenix Park, St Stephen's Green

PLACES OF WORSHIP
Christ Church Cathedral, St Mary's Pro-Cathedral, St Patrick's Cathedral

MUSEUMS
Dublin Writers' Museum, Heraldic Museum, Museum of Childhood, National Museum, Natural History Museum, Pearse Museum

OTHER ATTRACTIONS
Dublin Castle, Dublinia, Dublin's Viking Adventure, Dublin Zoo, James Joyce Centre, National Botanic Gardens, National Wax Museum, Trinity College

Connacht

THE ANCIENT KINGDOM of Connacht lies in the west of Ireland. Its jagged, mountainous west coast is divided from the rest of Connacht by a series of lakes.

The Shannon, the longest river in the British Isles, rises in northern Connacht and forms most of the border with Leinster to the east. It flows southwards through a chain of lakes and out into the Atlantic. Hundreds of small islands lie off the coast of Connacht.

▼ A Galway village
Leenane, on Killary Harbour, is famous for its woollen industry. There is even a Sheep and Wool Museum.

COUNTY FACTS

COUNTY GALWAY (CONTAE NA GAILLI
Area: 5,940 sq km
Population: 179,000
Administrative centre: Galway Cit
Other key places: Cleggan, Loughrea, Tuam

COUNTY LEITRIM (CONTAE LIARTHDRC
Area: 1,530 sq km
Population: 27,000
Administrative centre: Carrick-on-Shannon
Other key places: Leitrim

COUNTY MAYO (CONTAE MHUIGHE
Area: 5,400 sq km
Population: 116,000
Administrative centre: Castlebar
Other key places: Ballina, Ballyhaun Castlebar, Knock

Galway

Connemara, County Galway, is a mountainous region of peat bogs and thousands of small lakes. Part of it is a national park. Most people in this region live on small farms. Connemara ponies are bred here, and a form of limestone known as Connemara marble is mined. To the east is Lough Corrib, which extends almost to Galway City, the chief town of the county and an important industrial centre. The Aran Islands of Inishmore, Inisheer and Inishmaan are situated in Galway Bay.

▼ Wicker and tar
A curragh is a tiny Irish fishing boat. Traditionally it consists of a wicker frame that is made watertight with a covering of leather, canvas or tar.

▼ Pirate queen
Grace O'Malley was the daughter of a Connacht chief – and a notorious pirate during the 1500s. She had a fleet of pirate ships and her own castle on Clare Island, County Mayo.

Mayo, Sligo and Leitrim

Ireland's largest coastal island, Achill Island, lies to the south of Blacksod Bay, County Mayo. The island has a unique blend of sandy beaches, sheer cliffs, moorland and mountains. Two ranges, Slieve Gamph and the Ox Mountains, lie on the Mayo-Sligo border. Ireland's most famous poet, William Butler Yeats, is buried at Drumcliff in County Sligo, a place which inspired many of his poems. The northern part of County Leitrim is mountainous, while further south are low hills and valleys where the soil is poor.

Connacht and Roscommon

Connacht is farming country, with few large towns. County Roscommon is sandwiched between two rivers, the Shannon to the east and the Suck to the west. The land is boggy, but there is good grazing.

◀ Aran jumpers
Older inhabitants of the Aran Islands still wear traditional dress, including the famous Aran sweater. And many still speak Irish Gaelic as their first language.

COUNTY ROSCOMMON (ROS COMÁIN)
Area: 2,460 sq km
Population: 55,000
Administrative centre: Roscommon Town
Other key places: Boyle, Strokestown

COUNTY SLIGO (CONTAE SHLIGIGH)
Area: 1,800 sq km
Population: 56,000
Administrative centre: Sligo City
Other key places: Drumcliff, Easky

Moments in history

Perched on top of a sheer cliff on the Aran island of Inishmore is the spectacular prehistoric hill fort of Dun Aengus. The Aran Islands boast the remains of several forts, dating from the Iron Age through to the Middle Ages. The Kingdom of Connacht rose in importance under Niall of the Nine Hostages, who ruled at Tara, County Meath, from AD380 to 405. As *Árd Rí* (High King), Niall was ruler of all Ireland. His descendants held the title of *Árd Rí* until the Normans from England conquered Connacht in the 1200s.

▲ Dun Aengus

▼ **Red legs**
The rare chough is a relative of the all-black crow. It lives along the Galway coast.

G F E D C B A
7 6 5 4 3 2 1

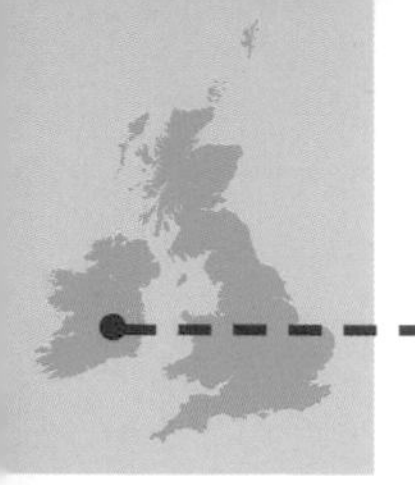

Leinster

LEINSTER IS THE LARGEST of Ireland's four provinces, consisting of a total of 12 counties. The province is famous for horse breeding and horse-racing: races have been held at the world-famous Curragh racecourse in County Kildare for around 2,000 years.

▼ **Fictional village**
The village of Avoca, in southern Wicklow, is the setting for the TV series *Ballykissangel*. Around 70,000 fans of the series make a pilgrimage to Avoca each year.

Leinster is surrounded by Ulster to the north, the Irish Sea to the east, Munster to the south and Connacht to the west. The coastline with the Irish Sea is far less jagged than Ireland's rugged west coast. Carlingford Lough, a long sea inlet, separates Leinster from County Down. Carlingford Mountain (590 metres) rises near the shores of the lough. The chief river of the province is the Liffey, which rises in the Wicklow Mountains, Leinster, and flows through the counties of Wicklow, Kildare and Dublin. Another important river is the Boyne, which rises in the Bog of Allen, County Kildare, and flows out into the sea at Drogheda, County Louth. The northern part of Leinster lies in the central plain of Ireland. There are areas of marshland in the northwest. The central plain continues south into the Bog of Allen. The Leinster Chain, a range which includes the Dublin, Wicklow and Blackstairs Mountains, runs down the east side of the region. Its highest point is Lugnaquillia (926 metres).

▼ **The Bog of Allen**
Bogs are dug for peat, which can be used as garden compost, or burnt as fuel.

Important towns

Dublin is the province's largest city. It is capital of the republic, and has an airport, port and university. Other important ports and industrial towns are Dunleary, Dundalk and Drogheda, in County Louth. The town of Wexford, in the southeastern corner of Leinster, is a seaport on the estuary of the river Slaney. Nearby Rosslare has an artificial harbour for large vessels and ferry services to Fishguard, in South Wales.

COUNTY FACTS

COUNTY CARLOW (CONTAE CEATHARACH)
Area: 895 sq km
Population: 40,958
Administrative centre: Carlow Town
Other key places: Leighlinbridge, Tullow

COUNTY DUBLIN (CONTAE ATHA CLEATH)
Area: 522 sq km
Population: 1,020,796
Administrative centres: Dublin, Dun Laoghaire
Other key places: Howth, Skerries

COUNTY KILDARE (CONTAE CHILL DARA)
Area: 1,695 sq km
Population: 116,015
Administrative centre: Naas
Other key places: Kildare Town, Newbridge

COUNTY KILKENNY (CONTAE CHILL CHOINNIGH)
Area: 2,060 sq km
Population: 73,094
Administrative centre: Kilkenny City
Other key places: Graiguenamanagh, Thomastown

COUNTY LAOIS (CONTAE LAOGHIS)
Area: 1,720 sq km
Population: 53,270
Administrative centre: Portlaoise
Other key places: Abbeyleix, Mountmellick, Portarlington

COUNTY LONGFORD
Area: 1,045 sq km
Population: 31,491
Administrative centre: Longford Town
Other key places: Lanesborough

▶ **Sky flier**
Sugar Loaf Mountain and Mount Leinster are popular with hang-gliders and paragliders.

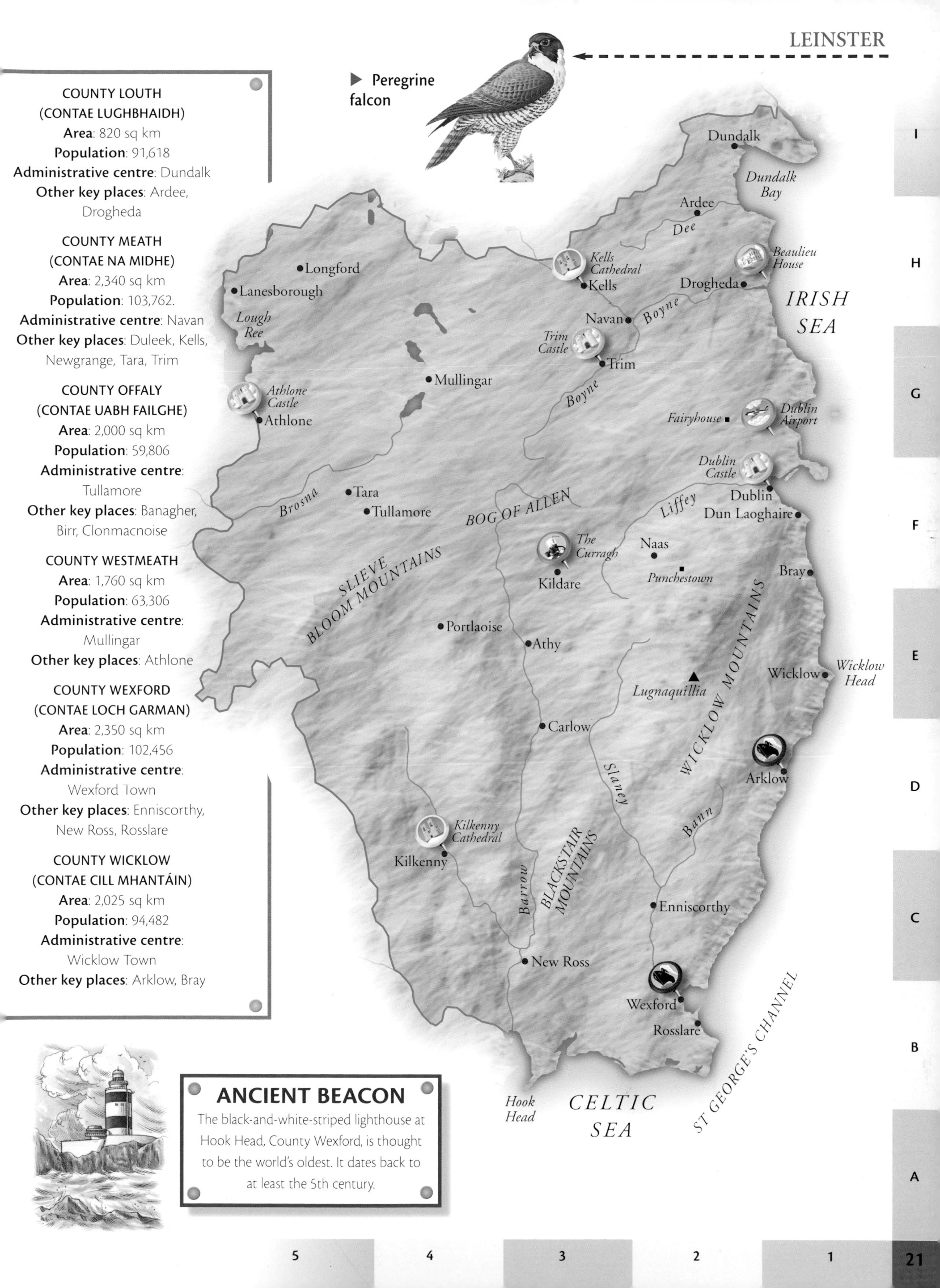

COUNTY LOUTH
(CONTAE LUGHBHAIDH)
Area: 820 sq km
Population: 91,618
Administrative centre: Dundalk
Other key places: Ardee, Drogheda

COUNTY MEATH
(CONTAE NA MIDHE)
Area: 2,340 sq km
Population: 103,762.
Administrative centre: Navan
Other key places: Duleek, Kells, Newgrange, Tara, Trim

COUNTY OFFALY
(CONTAE UABH FAILGHE)
Area: 2,000 sq km
Population: 59,806
Administrative centre: Tullamore
Other key places: Banagher, Birr, Clonmacnoise

COUNTY WESTMEATH
Area: 1,760 sq km
Population: 63,306
Administrative centre: Mullingar
Other key places: Athlone

COUNTY WEXFORD
(CONTAE LOCH GARMAN)
Area: 2,350 sq km
Population: 102,456
Administrative centre: Wexford Town
Other key places: Enniscorthy, New Ross, Rosslare

COUNTY WICKLOW
(CONTAE CILL MHANTÁIN)
Area: 2,025 sq km
Population: 94,482
Administrative centre: Wicklow Town
Other key places: Arklow, Bray

ANCIENT BEACON

The black-and-white-striped lighthouse at Hook Head, County Wexford, is thought to be the world's oldest. It dates back to at least the 5th century.

ONE OF THE BURIAL MOUNDS at Tara is believed to be around 4,000 years old. Kilkenny has the remains of several Stone Age tombs, and an Iron Age fort.

▲ Ancient remains
There are stunning Stone Age remains in County Meath at Dowth, Knowth and Newgrange.

In the early history of Ireland, part of Leinster formed a fifth province, or kingdom, called Meath. Stretching from the river Shannon to the Irish Sea, it included present-day Meath and Westmeath, but it was swallowed up in the Middle Ages. The High Kings of Ireland once ruled from the sacred hill of Tara, in modern-day County Meath. The kings were crowned on the Stone of Destiny, which was later kept at Westminster Abbey and is now in Scotland.

THE EASTER RISING

The British Government had promised that Ireland would have home rule in 1914, but they postponed its introduction because of the start of World War I. Impatient at the delay, on April 24th, 1916 (Easter Monday), a group of republicans started a rebellion in Dublin. Led by Patrick Pearse and Tom Clarke, they seized the General Post Office and other buildings. The uprising was suppressed at the cost of more than 400 lives, including 230 civilians. Fifteen rebel leaders were executed.

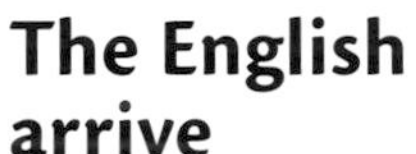

◀ The *Book of Kells*
The market town of Kells is an important religious site. There, monks produced the *Book of Kells*, one of the world's finest illuminated manuscripts. It is preserved at Trinity College, Dublin.

The English arrive

From 1042 the rulers of Leinster were members of the MacMurrough family. Dermot MacMurrough became king in 1126. His daughter, Eva, married a Norman baron, the Earl of Pembroke, nicknamed Strongbow. Dermot was banished from Ireland, and sought help from his son-in-law. Strongbow landed at Wexford, and with the aid of Norman allies conquered much of Ireland. This was the beginning of the English occupation of the island.

Castles

There are fine castles in Leinster, notably at Athlone, Ferns and Enniscorthy. Kilkenny City has a 12th-century castle and County Kildare boasts the ruins of more than 100 castles. Louth contains the ruins of several Norman castles. Many of the exploits of the mythical hero Cuchulain were supposed to have taken place in Louth.

◀ Battling it out
At the famous Battle of the Boyne in 1690, the Protestant William III finally defeated the Catholic James II, an event still celebrated by the Protestants of Northern Ireland.

WHAT'S IN A NAME?

Offaly was named King's County in 1556 after Philip II of Spain, the husband of Mary I of England. It resumed its ancient name in 1922. During the same period Laois was known as Queen's County, after Mary.

▼ **World-famous stout**

Guinness has been brewed in Dublin since 1759. This photo from the 1950s shows barrels of the stout being loaded on to barges on the Liffey.

Industry

Lanesborough, on Lough Ree, has a power station fuelled by peat. Laoise has a coalfield which produces anthracite. There is a large lead and zinc mine near Navan, and there are stone quarries across the province. Offaly has a variety of industries, mostly connected with agricultural produce. Arklow is an industrial town, with chemical plants.

Farming

Most of Leinster is devoted to agriculture. Farmers keep cattle, sheep and pigs. They grow cereal crops, potatoes, sugarbeet, fruit, vegetables and animal feed.

Fishing and horse-racing

The waters off the coast are rich fishing grounds. Catches include cod, herring and shellfish, such as lobsters and prawns. The National Stud of Ireland is at Tully, in County Kildare. Kildare is Ireland's flattest county – ideal for horse-racing. As well as the Curragh racecourse near Kildare Town, there are racecourses at Naas, Punchestown and Fairyhouse.

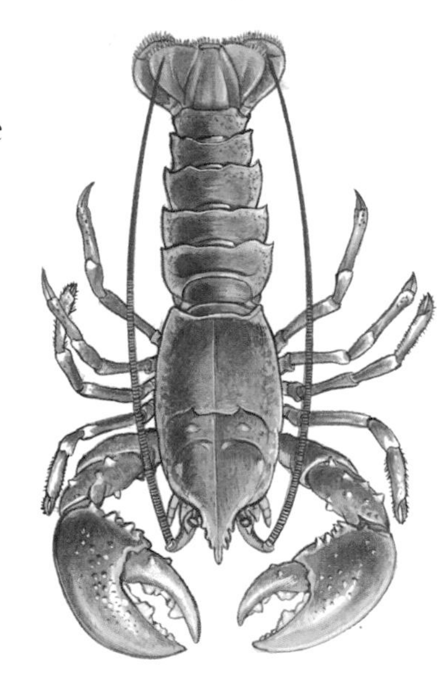

▲ **Food from the sea**

CAN YOU FIND?

1 Athlone Castle
2 Bog of Allen
3 The Curragh
4 Kells
5 Navan
6 Tara

see page 21

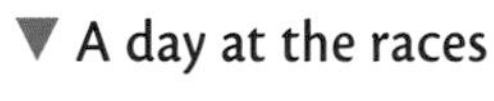

▼ **A day at the races**

Munster

COUNTY FACTS

COUNTY CLARE (CONTAE CHLÁIR)
Area: 3,188 sq km
Population: 91,343
Administrative centre: Ennis
Other key places: Lisdoonvara, Shannon, Spanish Point

COUNTY CORK (CONTAE CHORCAIGHE)
Area: 7,422 sq km
Population: 279,427
Administrative centre: Cork City
Other key places: Bantry, Blarney, Clonakilty, Mallow

▼ Wild landscape Killarney National Park, Kerry, covers 10,236 hectares.

MUNSTER COVERS THE SOUTHWEST of the island and occupies one-third of the Irish Republic. The province has scenic landscapes, including the beautiful Lakes of Killarney, which are one of Ireland's biggest tourist attractions.

Munster's coastline on the Atlantic Ocean is very rocky. Deep indents form numerous inlets and bays. County Limerick has a coastline on the Shannon Estuary. Around the town of Killarney in Kerry are the three Lakes of Killarney: Lough Leane, Muckross Lake and Upper Lake. Together with the surrounding woodland and Mountains of Kerry, they make up Killarney National Park. Munster consists mostly of moorland and highland, and includes the Republic's highest mountain, Carrauntoohil (1,040 metres), in the MacGillycuddy Reeks. From Limerick City, on the Shannon, running eastwards into County Waterford, is a region of rich, fertile farmland known as the Golden Vale. In the north of the province, County Clare forms a peninsula which is cut off from the rest of Munster by Lough Derg and the river Shannon.

▼ Swiss Cottage This gorgeous thatched cottage, surrounded by flowers, is in Cahir Park, County Tipperary. Its architect was John Nash, who also designed Regent's Park, London.

▼ Rare toad Natterjack toads can be found behind Inch Strand near Castle Gregory, County Kerry. The area is also home to the spotted Kerry slug.

Important towns

Most of Munster is rural, but more people live in the towns than in rural areas. County Kerry, the westernmost county of Ireland, has one of the largest groups of Gaelic speakers although their number is declining. The province's main towns are Cork, Waterford and Limerick. Both Cork and Waterford have good natural harbours – Cork Harbour is one of the finest in Europe. The Cove of Cork in the harbour is a naval base, dockyard and seaport. Waterford City is Ireland's largest container port. Shannon is a new town that has developed around Shannon International Airport.

▼ Rock of Cashel According to one legend, the huge Rock of Cashel in County Tipperary was bitten out of Devil's Bit Mountain by the devil himself. Cashel means 'fortress.'

▶ Clare's coast In County Clare the Cliffs of Moher, which have a sheer, 180-metre drop, run for about eight kilometres along the coast.

COUNTY KERRY
(CONTAE CHIARRAIGHE)
Area: 4,701 sq km
Population: 123,922
Administrative centre: Tralee
Other key places: Killarney, Listowel

COUNTY LIMERICK
(CONTAE LUIMNEACH)
Area: 2,667 sq km
Population: 107,963
Administrative centre: Limerick City

COUNTY TIPPERARY
(CONTAE THIOBRAD ÁRANN)
Area: 4,254 sq km
Population: 136,504
Administrative centres: Clonmel, Nenagh
Other key places: Cahir, Cashel, Tipperary Town

COUNTY WATERFORD
(PHORT LÁIRGE)
Area: 1,828 sq km
Population: 51,582
Administrative centre: Waterford
Other key places: Ardmore, Dungarvan

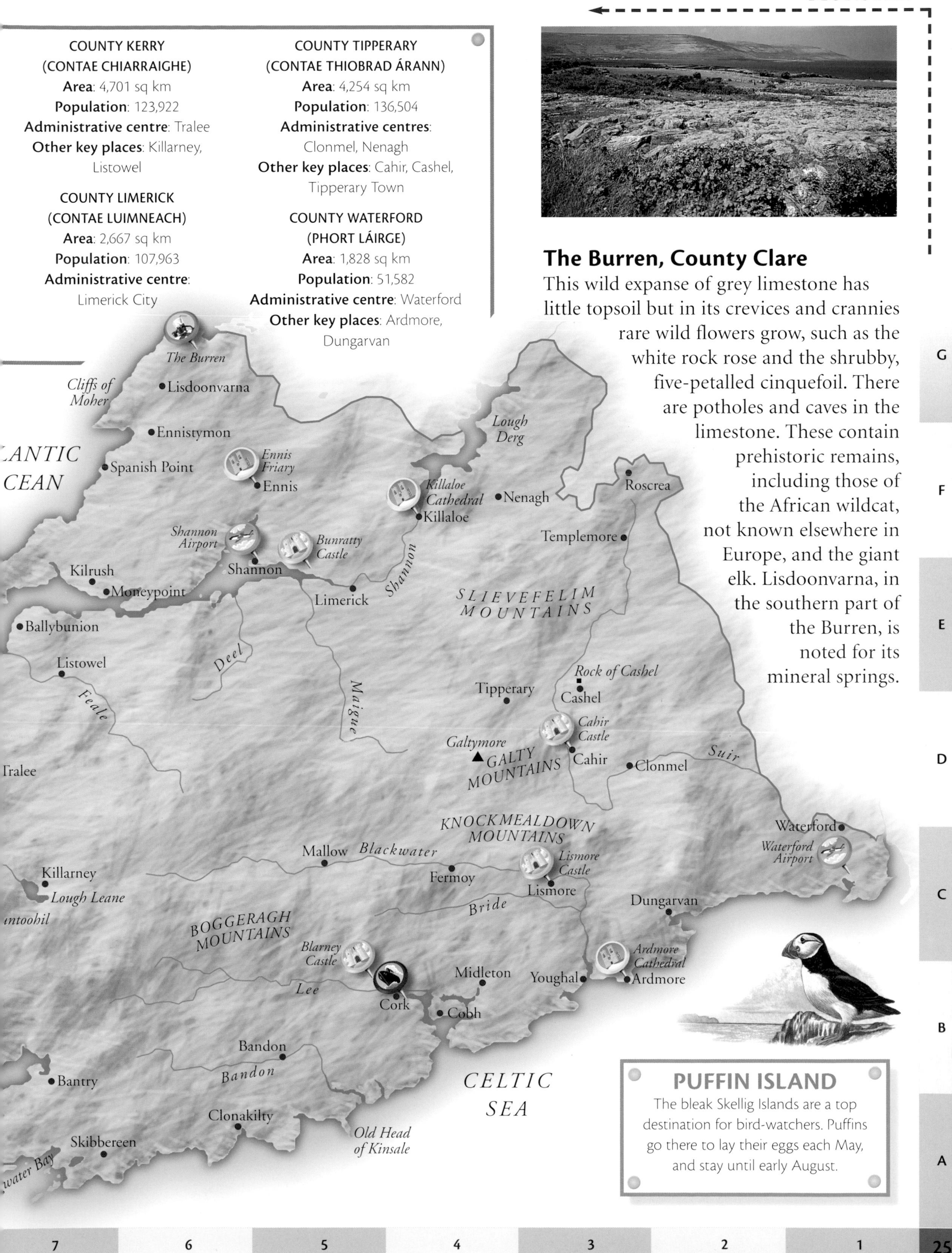

The Burren, County Clare

This wild expanse of grey limestone has little topsoil but in its crevices and crannies rare wild flowers grow, such as the white rock rose and the shrubby, five-petalled cinquefoil. There are potholes and caves in the limestone. These contain prehistoric remains, including those of the African wildcat, not known elsewhere in Europe, and the giant elk. Lisdoonvarna, in the southern part of the Burren, is noted for its mineral springs.

PUFFIN ISLAND

The bleak Skellig Islands are a top destination for bird-watchers. Puffins go there to lay their eggs each May, and stay until early August.

THE LITTLE MARKET TOWN OF BRUFF, about 25 kilometres south of Limerick City, was the site of the earliest-known farms in Ireland. Stone Age remains from around 3000BC have been found. There are Bronze Age remains in County Clare.

The medieval history of Munster began in the 5th century AD, when the region was divided into a number of small Christian kingdoms. Cashel was a stronghold of the ancient kings of Munster who were crowned there. Waterford was invaded in the 900s by the Vikings, who founded Waterford City, and in the 1100s by the Normans. Despite these invasions, the Irish people of the region have retained their identity, and the western part of the county is a stronghold of Gaelic speakers.

▲ **Sacred stones**
The first people settled in the Burren at the end of the Stone Age. They have left behind over 60 tombs.

THE BLARNEY STONE

According to legend, the triangular stone set into the wall of Blarney Castle, near Cork, has magical properties. Anyone who kisses it gains very strong powers of persuasion! The stone has been there since 1446.

▶ **Weaving history**
At Bunratty Folk Park, County Clare, there is a reconstructed traditional Irish village. There are working weavers, blacksmiths and butter-makers.

Castles

Lough Gurr, near Limerick City, has two ruined castles on its banks. They were originally built on artificial islands called crannogs. Most of what survives of Bunratty Castle, on the road between Limerick and Ennis, was built in the 1400s. Clare has a number of medieval round towers. The monastic site of Ardmore, County Waterford, has a fine round stone tower. Towers like this were used as watchtowers and as hiding places for monastic treasures. There is a castle at Lismore, on the river Blackwater. Cahir Castle, with its huge keep and large courtyard, dominates the small town of Cahir in County Tipperary.

◀ **At Spanish Point**
Ships of the Spanish Armada were wrecked off the coast of County Clare. At Cnoc na Crocaire (hill of the gallows), 60 Armada survivors were hung.

◀ Power provider
Moneypoint power station burns two million tonnes of coal each year. It supplies 40 percent of the country's electricity.

MUSIC AND DANCE

Traditional Irish dancing was made popular by the worldwide success of the dance show, *Riverdance*. Irish jigs are accompanied by folk music, usually performed by a simple quartet of musicians, who play the fiddle, tin whistle, a goat-skin drum called a *bodhrán*, and *uileann* pipes.

▼ Competitors, Irish dancing

Industry

Industry has grown up around the Limerick airport and the nearby city. There is a large oil refinery in Cork Harbour, and an offshore natural gasfield supplies people and industry in and around the city. Ireland's largest power station is coal-fired Moneypoint near the village of Killimer, County Clare. Other industries in County Cork are based on agriculture. Hunting, angling, climbing and tourism are important to Munster's economy. Another important industry is glass-making, centred in Waterford City.

Farming and wildlife

There is good farmland in the river valleys of Munster and on parts of the uplands, while large areas are rough pasture. Agriculture is the main activity, with the emphasis on rearing cattle, pigs and sheep. Potatoes, oats, wheat and sugarbeet are the main crops, plus beets called mangel-wurzels used for cattle feed.

▼ Waterford
Here, glass-blowers, cutters and engravers produce lead-crystal glassware that is world-famous.

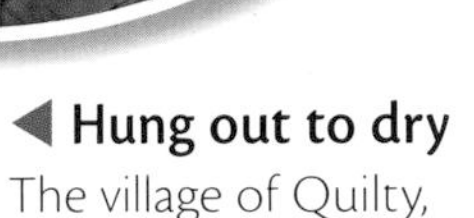

▲ Black pudding
The town of Clonakilty, County Cork, is famous for its delicious black pudding. This sausage is made from pigs' blood.

◀ Hung out to dry
The village of Quilty, County Clare, is a centre for seaweed production. Kelp and other marine plants are collected, dried and processed for use in toothpaste, beer, agar and cosmetics.

CAN YOU FIND?

1 Blarney Castle
2 The Burren
3 Clonakilty
4 Rock of Cashel
5 Spanish Point
6 Waterford

see pages 24 and 25

Ulster

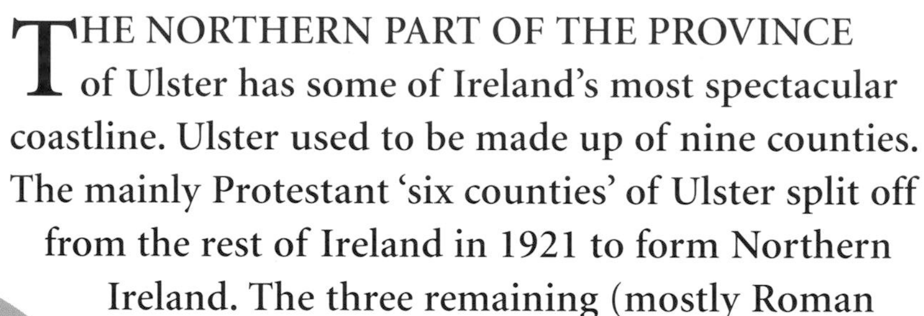

THE NORTHERN PART OF THE PROVINCE of Ulster has some of Ireland's most spectacular coastline. Ulster used to be made up of nine counties. The mainly Protestant 'six counties' of Ulster split off from the rest of Ireland in 1921 to form Northern Ireland. The three remaining (mostly Roman Catholic) Ulster counties formed part of the new, independent Republic of Ireland.

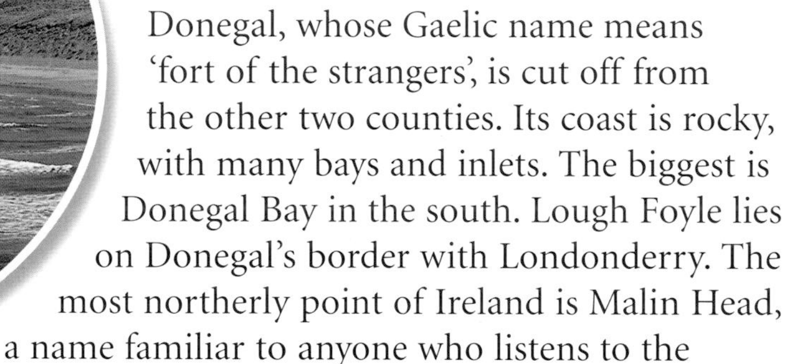

▼ **Donegal**
Donegal, on the Atlantic coast, has fine, sandy beaches and beautiful scenery.

Donegal, whose Gaelic name means 'fort of the strangers', is cut off from the other two counties. Its coast is rocky, with many bays and inlets. The biggest is Donegal Bay in the south. Lough Foyle lies on Donegal's border with Londonderry. The most northerly point of Ireland is Malin Head, a name familiar to anyone who listens to the shipping forecast. The Derryveagh Mountains and the Blue Stack Mountains are both in County Donegal, too. Further south, Cavan and Monaghan form part of Ireland's central plain of farmland. Cavan is crossed with uplands and deep valleys. Monaghan is a region of rolling hills, small lakes and peat bogs. Slieve Beagh is a bleak, boggy range of hills, rising to 383 metres.

▲ **Famine victims**
This statue commemorates the people who starved to death in the terrible Potato Famine (1845–9). The famine was caused by a fungus that spoilt the potato crop for several years running. Over a million people died and about 1.5 million emigrated.

▲ **Horse-riding in Donegal Bay**

▲ **Lace-making**
A traditional craft in Donegal is sewing delicate lace by hand.

Industry, farming and fishing

Donegal is highly-industrialized. Almost half the people work in textile or clothing factories, and many of the rest in service industries. Cavan and Monaghan have few large towns, but these have food-processing and clothing factories. Ulster farmers rear cattle, pigs and poultry and grow oats, barley and potatoes. Fishing is a flourishing industry.

◀ **Chicken**
Poultry is raised to provide eggs and meat.

◀ **Beehive hut**
This prehistoric stone hut is at Fahan, Donegal.

▶ **Rock pools**
The town of Bundoran is Donegal's most popular seaside resort.

COUNTY FACTS

COUNTY CAVAN
(CONTAE CABHÁN)
Area: 1,891 sq km
Population: 53,881
Administrative centre:
Cavan Town

COUNTY DONEGAL
(CONTAE DUN NA NGALL)
Area: 4,830 sq km
Population: 129,428
Administrative centre:
Lifford
Other key places:
Bundoran, Donegal, Killybegs

COUNTY MONAGHAN
(CONTAE MUINEACHÁN)
Area: 1,291 sq km
Population: 52,332
Administrative centre:
Monaghan Town
Other key places:
Castleblayney, Clones

Donegal tweed
Tweed is a rough, woollen cloth woven on a loom. Donegal is famous for the fabric and has its own unique pattern.

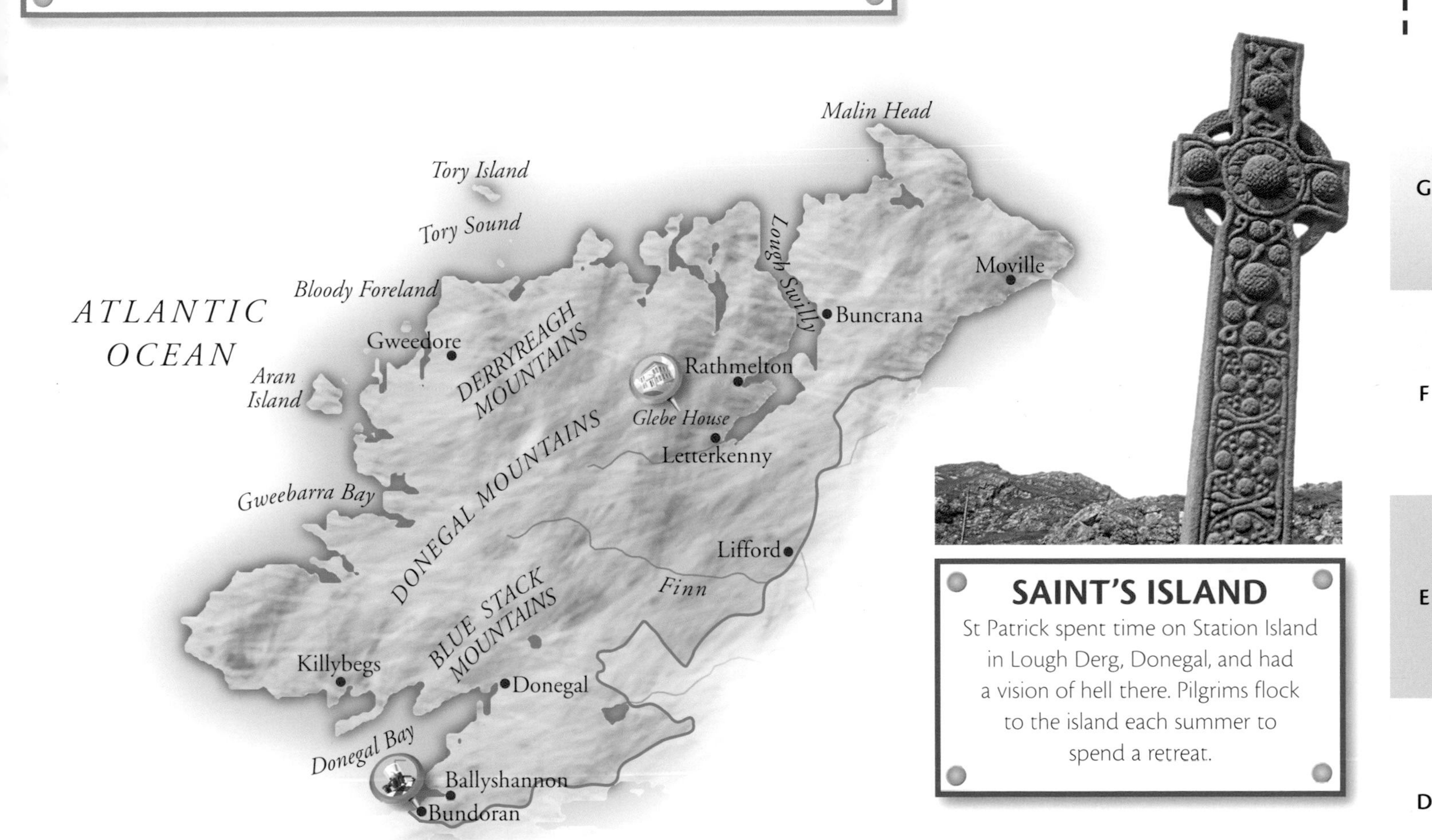

SAINT'S ISLAND

St Patrick spent time on Station Island in Lough Derg, Donegal, and had a vision of hell there. Pilgrims flock to the island each summer to spend a retreat.

Moments in history

Donegal's remoteness saved it from serious invasion by the Normans, and during the 1500s and 1600s fewer Scots and English settled here than in the more eastern parts of Ulster. It remained a stronghold of spoken Gaelic when other parts of Ireland were speaking English. Monaghan escaped being part of the plantation of Ulster because the English government had already divided its land among eight Irish chiefs. The populations of both Cavan and Monaghan were seriously reduced by the Potato Famine of 1845–9.

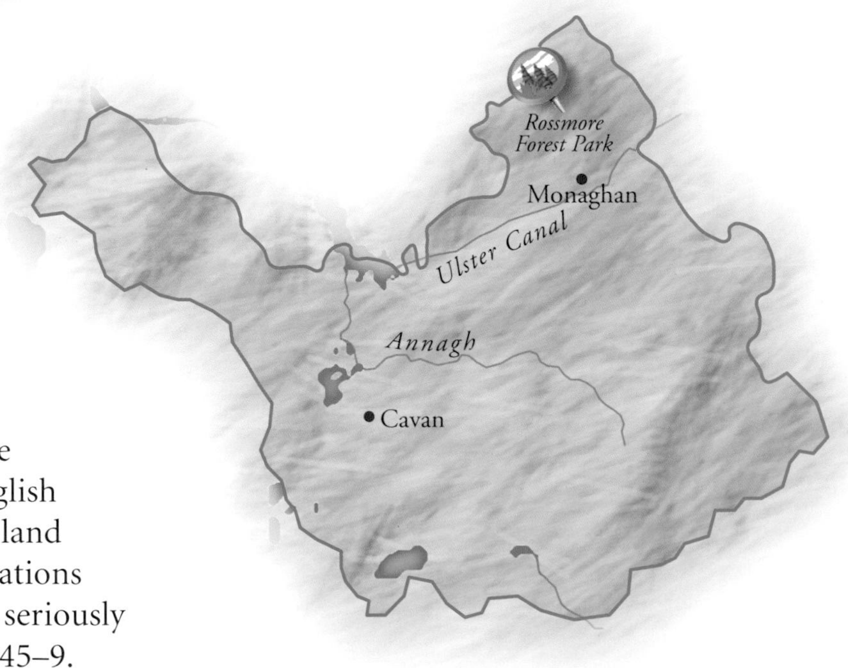

Glossary

Act of Union A law passed in parliament to join two (or more) countries together.

causeway A raised road or pathway, for example over marshy land, or across a stretch of sea.

distilling Process of purifying an alcoholic drink, such as whisky, by evaporating and condensing it.

dolmen A prehistoric stone structure, probably used as a tomb. It usually consisted of several standing stones with a flat stone placed on top.

earthwork A mound of earth used in prehistoric times as a fort.

erode To wear away the land. Wind, moving water and glaciers all erode the land.

escarpment The steep side of a hill, cliff or rock.

estuary The part of a river where it reaches the sea and often has tides; the river's mouth.

game Wild animals killed for food or sport, such as deer (for venison meat), geese or rabbits.

glacier A large sheet of ice, or ice and rock, that flows slowly down a valley like a frozen river.

gorge A deep, narrow canyon that cuts through the land.

granite A type of very hard, speckled igneous rock.

Gulf Stream Warm water current that originates in the Gulf of Mexico and flows across the Atlantic to northwestern Europe.

headland A point of land that juts out into the sea.

home rule Self-government, as opposed to rule by another country.

igneous Describes a rock formed when volcanic lava cooled. Granite and basalt are both igneous rocks.

inlet A small bay in a coastline.

islet A tiny island.

managed forest Trees planted rather like a crop to be harvested for their timber. Felled trees are replaced with new saplings.

medieval From the Middle Ages.

Middle Ages The time between the end of the Roman empire in the AD400s, until the explosion of invention and learning in the 1400s, known as the Renaissance.

national assembly An assembly of elected representatives that governs a country, or aspects of a country.

outcrop Rock that is visible at the surface, rather than hidden under the soil.

parliament The seat of government. Some members of parliament are elected by the people (in Britain, they attend the House of Commons; in the Republic of Ireland, they attend the Dáil); others are born or appointed to a position in the upper house (in Britain, this is the House of Lords; in the Republic of Ireland, this is the Senate).

patron saint A saint considered to be protector of a country.

peat bog Marshy land where peat has formed. Peat is long-decayed vegetation, the first step in the process that produces coal.

plantation of Ireland The settling of Ireland from the 1600s by English and Scottish people, so Britain could establish control.

plateau A area of level, high ground.

plug Rock that has hardened inside a volcano's central hole, or vent.

pothole A deep hole eroded in limestone.

prehistoric From the time before there were any written historical records.

prevailing wind The wind that blows most often in a particular place or region.

principality A territory ruled by a prince or princes.

Protestant Church A branch of Christianity that has separated from the Roman Catholic Church. Protestant churches first formed during the Reformation.

province A distinct part of a country, treated differently to the rest of the country.

refinery A place where raw ingredients are processed, for example an oil or sugar refinery.

regeneration The creation of new buildings and businesses in a place.

republic A country without a monarch as head of state, that is governed entirely by elected representatives of the people.

Roman Catholic Church The first Christian Church, headed by the Pope in Rome. Catholic means 'universal.'

rune A symbol that is a character, or letter, from one of the alphabets used by Germanic peoples between the 3rd and 13th centuries.

slate Shiny, green- or blue-grey rock made up of thin plates, often used for roofing tiles.

smallholding A small plot of land, usually used for farming.

solstice The day that the Sun is farthest away from the Equator. This happens twice in a year on the longest and shortest days, June 21st and December 21st.

stack An isolated pillar of rock, usually poking out of the sea.

standing stone A huge stone set upright in the ground. They were erected by prehistoric peoples, probably for religious purposes.

stone circle A ring of prehistoric standing stones.

suspension bridge A bridge with its deck supported from above by large cables or chains hanging from towers.

tributary A stream or river that flows into – and becomes part of – another, larger river.

tweed Rough, woollen cloth. Much of it is produced in the valley of the river Tweed.

wetland Marshy land.

MAP CO-ORDINATES

Co-ordinates provide a way to find a place on a map. On each map page there is a border at the bottom that is divided into numbered blocks, and a border at the edge that is divided into lettered blocks. Together with the page number, these border numbers and letters are used to create the co-ordinates.

1 Write down the page that the place is on. This is the first co-ordinate. If you want co-ordinates for Galway then '19' is the first part, because Galway appears on the map on page 19.
2 Next put your finger on the place itself. Trace down to the bottom of the page and see which numbered block you reach. This number is the second co-ordinate. In the case of Galway, you reach number '4'
3 Now put your finger back on the place and trace across to the edge of the page to see which lettered block you reach. This is the last co-ordinate. In the case of Galway, you reach letter 'B.'
4 Write down the three co-ordinates, separating them with commas so that they don't get muddled together. The co-ordinates for Galway would be '19, 4, B.'

Index

Numbers in *italics* refer to illustrations.

A
Achill Island 18
Act of Union 6, 17
agriculture 27
aircraft factory 10
Anglo-Irish agreement 7
Antiphonary of Bangor 14
Antrim 13, 15
Aran Islands 18, 19
  sweaters *18*
Árd Rí (High King) 19
Armada *26*
Armagh 13, 15
Avoca *20*

B
Ballykissangel 20
Bangor 14
Bann river 12
basalt 9
Battle of the Boyne 22
beehive hut *28*
beer 23
Belfast 10–11, 12
  Belfast Castle *10*
  Botanic Gardens *11*
  City Hall 10, *11*
  Custom House *10*
  Donegall Square 10, *11*
  Lagan river *11*
  places of interest 11
  Queen's Bridge *10*
  Stormont Castle 10, *11*
  Ulster Museum 10
Belfast District 13
Belfast Lough 10
Belleek pottery 15
bird-watching 13, 25
black pudding 27
Blarney Stone 26, *26*
Bog of Allen *20*
Book of Kells 17, *22*
Boyne river 20
brewing *23*
Bruff 26
Bunratty Folk Park *26*
Burren, The *9*, 25, *26*

C
Cahir Castle 26
Cahir Park *24*
Carlingford Lough 20
Carlingford Mountains 20
Carrauntoohil 24
Carrick-a-Rede rope bridge 15
Cashel 26
Castle Gregory 24
Chichester, Sir Arthur 11
chough *19*
Clarke, Tom 22
Cliff of Moher *24*
climate 9
Clonakilty *27*
clothing 28
Connacht 18–19
Connemara 18
  marble 18
  ponies 18
Cork (Town) 24
County Antrim 13
County Armagh 13
County Carlow 20
County Cavan 28, 29
County Clare 24
County Cork 24
County Donegal *8*, *28*, 29
County Down *12*, 13, 15
County Dublin 20
County Fermanagh 13, 15
County Galway 18
County Kerry 24, 25
County Kildare 20
County Kilkenny 20, 22
County Laois 20, 23
County Leitrim 18
County Limerick 25
County Londonderry 13
County Longford 20
County Louth 21
County Mayo 18
County Meath 21, *22*
County Monaghan 28, 29
County Offaly 21, 23
County Roscommon 18, 19
County Sligo 18, 19
County Tipperary 25
County Tyrone 13, 15
County Waterford 25
County Westmeath 21
County Wexford 21
County Wicklow 21
Courci, John de 11
Cromwell 15, 17
Cuchulain 7, *7*, 14, 22
curragh 18
Curragh racecourse 20, 23, *23*
currency 7

D
Dáil Éireann 6
distilleries
  Bushmills *15*
Donegal 28, 29
Dublin 16–17, 20, 22
  bridges *16*
  cathedrals 16
  Custom House 16, *16*
  DART (Dublin Area Rapid Transport) *17*
Dublin Castle 16
  Government Buildings *16*
  history 17
  Leinster House 6
  Liffey river *17*
  O'Connell Street 16
  Parnell Square *17*
  places of interest 17
  St Patrick's Cathedral 16, *16*
  Trinity College 16, *17*, *22*
Dun Aengus 19, *19*
Dunseverick Castle 15

E
Eire 6
Emerald Isle *8*, 9
English Civil War 12
English Pale 17

F
farming 15, 23, 27, 28
fishing 23, 28
Free State 6

G
Gaelic 7, 18, 24, 29
gasfield 7
Giant's Causeway 9, *9*, 12
glaciers *9*
glass-making *27*
Golden Vale 24
Gortin Glen Forest Park 13
Guinness *23*

H
Henry II 6, 17
history 6, 14
Home Rule 6
Hook Head lighthouse *21*
horse breeding and racing *20*, 23
hydroelectric power station 15

I
industry 15
Inishmore 19
IRA (Irish Republican Army) 7
Irish dancing *27*
Irish harp *6*
Irish Sea 8, 9

J
James II 22

K
Killarney National Park 24, *24*
Kingdom of Connacht 18, 19
Kingdom of Ulster 14
Knights of the Red Branch 14

L
lace-making *28*
Lagan river 10
Lakes of Killarney 24
languages 7, 18, 24, 29
Laois 23
Leenane *18*
Legananny Dolmen 14
Leinster 20–23
Liffey river 16, *17*, 20
lighthouse *21*
linen weaving 10, 11, *15*
Londonderry 12, *12*, 15
Londonderry City District 13
Lough Corrib 18
Lough Derg 24
Lough Foyle 28
Lough Neagh 8, 12

M
MacCool, Finn *12*
MacGillycuddy Reeks 24
MacMurrough, Dermot 6, 22
MacNessa, Conor 14
Malin Head 28
Mary I of England *23*
Meath 22
mining 23
Mount Stewart House 12
mountains 8, 18
Mountains of Antrim 12
Mourne Mountains 12, *12*
Munster 24–27

N
natterjack toad *24*
Niall of the Nine Hostages 14, 19
Northern Ireland 7, 12–15
northern pike *8*

O
Offaly 23
oil refinery 27
O'Malley, Grace *18*
Orangemen *14*

P
patron saint 6, 16
Pearse, Patrick 22
peat bogs 8, 10, *23*
Philip II of Spain *23*
physical features 8–9
pilgrims 29
plantation of Ireland 14
plantation of Ulster 29
Potato Famine 28, 29
power stations 23, *27*
Protestants 6, 14
provinces 6
puffins *25*

Q
Quilty *27*

R
racecourse see Curragh
religions 7
Republic of Ireland 6, 7
Rock of Cashel *24*
rocks 8, 9
Roman Catholics 6, *7*, 14
Rosslare 20

S
St Patrick *6*, *14*, 29
seaweed *27*
shamrock *6*
Shannon 8, *8*, 18, 24
shipbuilding 10
Skellig Islands 25
Slieve Beagh 28
Slieve Donard 12
Spanish Point 26
Sperrin Mountains 12, 13
Station Island *29*
Stone Age 14, *22*
Stone of Destiny 22
Strangford Lough 13
Strongbow 6, 22

T
Tara 19, 22
terrorism 7
textiles 28
Titanic 10
Torr Head 8
tweed 29

U
Ulster 28–29

V
Vikings 6, 16

W
Waterford 24, 26, *27*
Wexford 20
whiskey see distilleries
Wicklow Mountains 8, *9*
wild flowers 25
wildlife 13
William III 22

Y
Yeats, William Butler 18

Acknowledgements

The publishers would like to thank the following artists whose work appears in this title:

Lisa Alderton/Advocate,Vanessa Card, Kuo Kang Chen; Wayne Ford, Terry Gabbey/AFA Ltd., Jeremy Gower, Ron Hayward, Gary Hincks, Sally Holmes, Richard Hook/Linden Artists,The Maltings, Janos Marffy, Terry Riley, Andrew Robinson, Peter Sarson, Mike Saunders, Christian Webb/Temple Rogers, Mike White/Temple Rogers, John Woodcock

PHOTOGRAPHIC CREDITS

The publishers thank the following sources for the use of their photographs

6 (T/L) Huntingdon Library & Art Gallery, San Marino, CA, USA/Bridgeman Art Library; (B/L) Bettmann/Corbis, 7 (T/L) Hulton Deutsch/Corbis, (C) S.Rafferty/Eye Ubiquitous/Corbis, (B/L) Private collection/Bridgeman Art Library: 9 (B/R) Tom Bean/Corbis; 10 (B/L) Michael St.Maur Sheil/Corbis, (T/R & T/C) from BSK Photo Library, (C/L) Sean Sexton Collection/Corbis; 11 (T/L) BSK Photo Library; 12 (C/R) & (B/L) A.Davis/Leslie Garland Picture Library, (B/R) J.Harpur/The National Trust Photographic Library; 14 (B/R) North Down Heritage Centre; (B/L) AFP/Corbis; 15 (T/L) Reproduced by kind permission of the Trustees of the National Museums & Galleries of Northern Ireland, (B/C) Bushmills; 16 (T/R) & (B/R) BSK Photo Library; 17 (C/R) BSK Photo Library,(T/R) Skyscan Photo Library; 17 (B/L) Iarnrod Eireann 18 (B/R) Abbie Enock/Travel Ink; 19 ((T/R) K.Dwyer/Skyscan Photo Library; 20 (C/L) A.Davies/Leslie Garland Picture Library; 22 (C/R) Hulton-Deutsch/Corbis; 23 (B) Creative Imprints, 23 (T/R) Guinness Ltd. 24 (T/L) K.Dwyer/Skyscan, (C/R) Jill Swainson/Travel Ink; 25 (T/L) Ken Gibson/Travel Ink; 26 (T/L) K.Dwyer/Skyscan Photo Library; 27 (T/L) Moneypoint Power Plant, (C) Brian Lynch/Bord Failte, (B/R) K.Dwyer/Skyscan Photo Library, (C/R) Irish Dancing Magazine; 28 (T/R), (C/L) Brian Lynch/Bord Failte, (B/R) Erne Enterprise Development Co. Ltd./Bundoran UDC; 29 (T/R) Abbie Enock/Travel Ink.

Every effort has been made to trace and credit all images used and the publishers apologise if any have been omitted.

All other photographs from MKP Archives.

'CAN YOU FIND?' answers

Ireland: Northern Ireland p15

1	Armagh	13, 4, B
2	Belfast	13, 2, C
3	Bushmills	13, 3, E
4	Downpatrick Cathedral	13, 2, B
5	Slieve Donard	13, 2, A

Ireland: Leinster p22

1	Athlone Castle	21, 5, G
2	Bog of Allen	21, 4, F
3	The Curragh	21, 3, F
4	Kells	21, 3, H
5	Navan	21, 3, H
6	Tara	21, 5, F

Ireland: Munster p27

1	Blarney Castle	25, 5, B
2	The Burren	25, 6, G
3	Clonakilty	25, 6, A
4	Rock of Cashel	25, 3, E
5	Spanish Point	25, 7, F
6	Waterford	25, 1, C